SONGS FROM A MONSOON SWING AND Other Poems

BY LAVANYA DEEPAK SHAH

SONGS FROM A MONSOON SWING
And Other Poems
By

Lavanya Deepak Shah

Setu Publications
* Pittsburgh, PA (USA) *

© 2020 by Lavanya Deepak Shah

All rights reserved. No part of this work may be reproduced, translated, recorded, stored, transmitted, or displayed in any form, or by any means electronic, mechanical, or otherwise without the prior written permission of the author, the copyright owner except for brief quotations in book reviews, and as otherwise permitted by applicable law. Any such quotations must acknowledge the source.

We would be pleased to receive email correspondence regarding this publication or related topics at setuedit@gmail.com.

ISBN-13 (paperback): 978-1-947403-08-6
Cover Art: Watercolor by Smt. Sushila Narendra Sharma
Printed and bound in the United States of America.
Distributed to the book trade worldwide by Setu Publications, Pittsburgh (USA)

Although every precaution has been taken in the preparation of this work, neither the author nor the publisher shall have any liability to any person or entity with respect to any loss or damage caused or alleged to be caused directly or indirectly by the information contained in this work.

Setu Literary Publications, Pittsburgh, USA

SONGS FROM A MONSOON SWING

By

Lavanya Deepak Shah

DEDICATION

Want to dedicate this English book of poems to all my children: son in law Brian McRedmond, daughter Sindur and their son Noah, our son Sopan, daughter in law Monica and their son Orion.

SONGS FROM A MONSOON SWING
And Other Poems

By

Lavanya Deepak Shah

Acknowledgement

I thank Shri Anurag Sharma cordially for staying on this lyrical journey with me and guiding me gently thus helping me in fulfilling this project. Many of my poems, have been written at different times of my life. Today they are in one place. They have taken a proper shape in the form of a book of poems. For me, it was a long-cherished dream to see all my English poems in one place! I'm glad to see my first collection of English poems titled: "*Songs from a Monsoon Swing and Other Poems*" finally in a book form! Those loose leafed poems, scattered on wings of time and recessed in the vastness of infinite space, could not have taken a physical form without Anurag Sharma's guidance and technical know-how! That is the truth and I thank him profusely.

Beyond all his glittering achievements, I consider him my younger brother and I've found him to be the most sincere human being. He says what he means and also means what he says. So, you get what you see from his honest personality which is rare in these modern complex times. I thank him for his unselfish gesture in presenting this book which I hope all of you, my wonderful readers, will enjoy.

SONGS FROM A MONSOON SWING

Table of Contents

Preface	11
Good Wishes Message	15
Abhisarika (By Smt. Susheela Sharma)	17
Songs from a Monsoon Swing	19
Love Travels	40
Eulogy	41
Your Name	43
I Will Return (JE REVINS)	44
Night Traveler	45
Rose Bush	46
Rain	47
Memories My Love	48
Seasons	49
Memories	51
Always	53
Spirit	55
All Alone Without You	57

Diwali	58
Me, and my Fisher Woman!	59
Sword	62
Conversation	64
Love is Immortal	67
India	72
Ah Hope!	75
America (A Prayer)	79
Love	81
Aah! the gypsy sings	83
About Long Poem	85
Cover Artist	87
Author's Biodata	89

Preface

The parched and hot landmass of India awaits eagerly for the arrival of life-giving relief in form of the monsoon rains. The Monsoons are large-scale sea breezes which occur when the temperature on land is significantly warmer or cooler than the temperature of the ocean. Indian Monsoon season runs from June to September.

The monsoon and rain laden clouds do not appear all at once! Rather, they build up slowly over a couple of days as tip toeing gently, they enter as delightful "pre-monsoon showers." Monsoon's actual arrival is announced by much fanfare as an intense period of heavy rain as it unleashes over the Hot coastal plains of India.

The sky is lit up with booming thunder and intense lightning strikes the grey skies. The heavy rain droplets inject relief from heat and dust infusing an amazing amount of vigor into people.

On streets and alleys children run about shouting and screaming with joy as they dance in the streets soaking the pouring rain and play merry games.

Even the adults join in fun because the Monsoon break is so refreshing!

There is a custom in India to tie up thick ropes on stout branches of sturdy trees and create swings for the females of a village or cities to enjoy this Monsoon season. They enjoy the outdoors among nature interacting with the balmy monsoon breeze. Scorched Earth sprinkled with the fresh raindrops lets out a most wonderful fragrance into the air as the first gentle raindrops hit the hot parched earth! It is an unforgettable experience to witness the arrival of Monsoon on Indian plains.

The women swing into action in singing songs of welcome and joy! They laugh and play with each other as they enjoy their sport on monsoon swings.

Many girls arrive from distant towns or villages to their paternal homes to enjoy few days of respite. To enjoy monsoon swings is an age-old ritual.

An age-old scene from the ancient land of India comes alive!

There are festivals like Hariyalee Tej celebrated all over Northern parts of India. This Festival of Teej falls on the third day of the first fortnight of the Hindu lunar month of Shravan. Teej is indeed a joyous time for the ladies. It's a time to get together with family and friends. It is time to put aside everyday worries for a while and relax among other female friends.

In many North Indian states like Punjab, Rajasthan and Uttar Pradesh, grand processions of decorated idols of Hindu Mother Goddess Parvati and her husband Lord Shiva are carried out in streets by thousands of devotees with musical drumbeats. Elephants, camels and dance folks and acrobats perform side by side as numerous artists join in such a grand procession. Teej festival is a day widely celebrated by married Hindu women in northern and western parts of India to pray for the long life and well-being of their husbands.

Many villages, towns and helmets beautifully decorate swings and hang them on age old village trees, in open places so they can be enjoyed by anyone. Some other major activities include shopping, singing, dancing and palm decoration with henna.

In this long poem titled 'Songs from a Monsoon Swing' a similar scene is conjured up for a modern world reader to get familiar with this ancient rhythm of life cycle. Regeneration, restfulness and then sport and activities makes our human life form reach fruition as it reinforces emotional ties and strengthens cultural bonds and the circle of life reaches its completion.

Every year as the monsoon season surely arrives with certainty, the faith in life regains strength and forms new bonds that form along with the securely tied strings of each swing and the strong ropes on sturdy branches of ancient trees beckon the familiar faces to be part of this merriment.

The festivities and fun unfurl as genuine smiles on faces of simple folks.

The young turn old and old customs gain strength. Perpetuating life itself. Life's transient nature is glimpsed through this shiny prism of light thus in these poetic verses, as the women gathered at their monsoon swing exchange tidbits and trivia about their mundane lives. Under the shade of ancient Banyan Trees, on swaying swings on a monsoon breeze the songs erupt. Some are happy, some are melancholy and some expectant while some are old and wise. They exchange their thoughts with each other.

There is a silent spectator to this magical scene! A young shepherd boy who witnesses this scene in awe! As an incarnation of each reader's inner eye, the shepherd boy's watchful eyes witness the unfolding song of life and the song of monsoon swing comes alive.

There are additional poems also in this small book. I hope you will like '*The songs from a Monsoon Swing and Other Poems*'.

Lavanya Deepak Shah

Atlanta (Georgia), and Ohio, USA

Good Wishes Message

'*Songs from a Monsoon Swing and Other Poems*' is a captivating collection of poems by Lavanya Shah. It comprises of the long poem 'Songs from a Monsoon Swing' that is a recollection of magical moments of her life, and many other songs of memory, love, and wistfulness. The power of her poetry comes from its directness, balance, and use of subtle imagery. She speaks of emotion in a manner that takes us beyond the immediate context to deeper intuitions about the paradoxes of life. This book deserves a wide audience.

Subhash Kak
Department of Electrical and Computer Engineering
Louisiana State University, Baton Rouge, LA 70803-5901

Subhash Kak's research is on cybersecurity, artificial intelligence, quantum computing, archaeoastronomy, and history of science. He is a member of Indian Prime Minister's Science, Technology and Innovation Advisory Council (PM-STIAC) since 2018. He was awarded the Indian civilian award Padma Shri in 2019.

Abhisarika (By Smt. Susheela Sharma)

Songs from a Monsoon Swing

As the blue sky turns gray

The Maidens come out to play

Laughing and running, they come,

Over green grass, as they run,

Their feet patter as they pass-

One holds another's hand

Pulling her to where she stands!

The 'Neem' tree, sways wildly in breeze

The flower decked swing on 'Banyan' swings!

Soon others follow their lead

The sensuous fragrance of Earth

Fill their nostrils; it flares as they play-

A diamond twinkles on a shapely nose-

The saffron sari, makes sails in the wind,

These are the Monsoon winds of Hind!

Laden with the smell of spices, they weigh

Like a serpent's hiss, mingled with 'sandal wood kiss!'

The girls of sixteen, seventeen or twenty
Playful, graceful as nature meant-
Red marks on forehead, kohled eyes
Limber limbs that go flashing by—
It's a hoard of young maidens
Has heaven descended upon earth?

The sky with streaks of pink,
Salmon, amber, red and yellow delights!
Their fabrics flutter in the breeze
Some green, purple and some gold
The small tight 'cholis' cling so light,
Trying to hold their sallow breath!

Red pouting lips then part,
Ruby red tongue on lips then darts,
Small white teeth glimmer and shimmer,
Like pearls of wisdom caged within!

Long hair, pleated and parted, hangs till the waist
An orchid near ear hides like a fond guest.
Ears adorned with gold, look like shells,
Hearing sounds of cuckoos and tinkling bells!

The carefree run of young maidens,
Who have come visiting their parents,
They are back to grace their childhood Homes!
Oh! It's a divine pleasure, to roam —

"My lover awaits far away," says one,
"I have just begun here my stay,
I miss him at nights, my dear,
But the days seem alright, if I may say!"
"Don't listen to our talks, young girl!

"You have yet to await your turn!"
Thus, said an elderly and wise,
'Oh, how wonderful it is, oh! So nice!"

The conversation, the light hearty banter,
Of hearts, filled with love, clear in its candor,
So many generations have thus passed-
From bloom to bloom in dust so fast!
As the Monsoon winds bring the rain,

The sky turns Grey, Peacock turns vain,
He dances with muddy feet and gazes,
The gathering of dark clouds up there!
The peahen longingly gazes,
The peacock's eyes then brims at its rim,
The tears spill on the dusty hot ground,
The feathers, brilliant, swirl, in passion around!

A fawn comes running by from somewhere,
At the doe eyed damsel's eyes it gazes
Then it darts among the wooded hills,
Nature then vibrates and thrills!

The anklets of silver and bangles of gold,
On slender limbs it's a joy to behold!
Silk skirts flap, in a stormy breeze,
And clutches a youth's heart, in a squeeze!
Ah! The dark, dimpled "Shephard Boy",

His locks abandoned in careless joy
Leans forward on his staff and stares,
At the horde of women, intent on their play!

His white teeth, flashes in a smile
The girl who was last, smiles, beguiled
Her companion pulls her forward
"Stay with us friend," she chides!

The one who was last, turns swiftly and waves
To the youth, staring at her, he just stares!
Dear God! Was it a dream that I saw!
Were they going where I thought?"

Thinking such thoughts, he stares,
And scratching at his hair he says,
"It is Monsoon winds that blow,
O maidens! Why don't you walk slow!"

"Wet is the Earth! Wet is the sky!
Wet is the wind, passing us by!
Wet are the leaves lush on trees,
Wet are birds, silently sailing on wings!
Wet are the petals of flowers in bloom

Some dewdrops slip its way in a bud's bosom!
The butterfly is imprisoned; its wings are stuck!
Green frogs are leaping on Lotus leaf amuck!
The lotus gathers rainwater, holds it like a cup
The bee has come, wanting to Sup,
The lily pond gathers, the first big drops,

As doves and pigeons gather in droves!
Quiet is the Earth, in an expectant hush,

The scorched dust will turn to slush
The smell of earth will then fill the bough
Where the maidens are headed now!

Let me go and watch them play
On the Monsoon swings as they will sway!
It's a feast for my eyes—and food for my thirsty soul O my!"
Saying thus to his white and black sheep
Carrying a lamb, tight in his limbs,
The boy follows the rushing group of girls
Who are about to play, dance and swirl!
As the opening nears, the chatter arises,
The girls run for their first turns,
On the monsoon swings they swing,
With falling rain, they dance, whirl and sing!

The Monsoon swings now come into view,
Hanging from stout ancient Banyan limbs
Fragrant flowers' garlands entwines,
On both strands of strings, on both sides!

As tiny soft palms, crush the flowers

Clutching at the strings, holding within,

The limber limbs climb high on swings,

Then laughter in all directions rings!

"Push it up! Push it up to the sky!"

"Watch it, watch it! I'll fall, O MY!"

The screaming and shouting in joust,

Rises in unison, as they shout!

The shepherd boy now gazes in awe,

At the wonderful sight that at bough saw,

A sight that is straight from Heavens Oh!

"Why a mere mortal like me, is that who saw!"

The lamb then slips away from his grasp

And the lad in agony then gasps,

"Mai, ma i' it limbers on and cries,

As it runs ahead on the path and shies!

"Look, who comes to join us at our play!"

Says a young girl pouting in mock dismay-

As her gaze falls on the boy shepherd,
She mischievously calls all to gather—
She points out the boy, hiding out there,
Her friends laugh and then snare,
"He will be punished for his crime,
He watched us hidden, that's not right!"
The bold one advances ahead then,
Catches the boy to make him a man,
He is surrounded by a bevy of girls,
Some are married, some still hidden as pearls!

They tear his clothes and beat his chest,
The frail arms, like creepers, sways and rest.
The Boy, shields himself up yet smiles,
"God is kind to me" he mimes, rolling his eyes!

His dark cheeks draw in a soft dimple,
His strong arms and wide chest is now nimble,
Then another girl, brings forth a summer garland,
Of marigold, strung together, on his neck lands!

The boy pulls one of the girls to his chest!
It's the 'last one' that had strayed on the path
A maiden, coy and shy, he pulls in embrace,
She flutters in his grip, like a frightened dove!
He swiftly kisses her, on her Ruby lips,
And breaks the circle of others' arms—
A stolen kiss, from a sweet sixteen,
He will remember forever, this Monsoon swing!
He runs away, agile as a panther loose,
The girls give up their futile chase,
It was but an 'Interlude', in their game!!

'Let's get with our play, they then say.
The young, shy girl of sweet sixteen,
Still stands there, trembling from head to feet,
"O mercy me! What he did to me!
"In front of all my friends, to see!"
Do my eyes look different now?
Do my lips look quite pale?
Do I walk now in a different way?

Oh! He was such a naughty male!
The others laugh at her discomfort
They admonish her then to forget-
"Such things happen, here, my love!

When Monsoon clouds roll thundering by!"
Now their games begin in earnest
There will be no rest now for the swings!
One by one, they climb on the plank
Sandalwood smell emerges as they swing!
The swing goes high now, now low,
Two girls, in pairs, ride fast and slow!
Face to face, they straddle the plank,
Their arms and fingers, clutching the strand!
They shift their weight sometimes,
And bend slightly from their waist,
The swings gather great momentum
Swaying to and fro, like a pendulum!

"How still seems the sky above?

How still the earth beneath!
How we seem suspended in sky,
In a timeless motion", they think!
As the pairs of exuberant girls, whirl,
Holding out their hands, round they twirl!
In a rhythmic motion-in semi-circle,
Their feet making patterns below in dust------
Now laughing, now playing and panting,
They stop just to hold their breaths,
As their heads swim in a daze!
But laughter still from throat escapes---

A sister sings alone a sad song—
And calls to her brother near in her song.
"O brave brother of mine! Come soon,
It is upon me again, Monsoon!"
So many girls have come visiting,
To their father's homes, it's homecoming!
Why have you yet not come for me?
I pine to be home, I know, you will!"

"O father mine! Have you forgotten me -?
"Why didn't you send my brother for me?"
"O my mother, I still feel your touch,
"When I touch my hair, it pains me so much!"
"I have come so far away from you—
"You sent me far away from Home!
To love and to cherish, to honor and serve,
My husband's family, as that is the norm!"

"In this world, there is just one sin!
"That's to be born as a woman in Hind!
A daughter, a wife, a sister or mother,
Only to give and give, silently and give"

The haunting song and the sad melody,
Stops the swinging girls in their tracks!
They come near her and gather her at bosom,
And one by one, every eye tears, then sheds!

A wife of one is a daughter of some,

A woman changes, so many forms—

She is the silent bridge of humanity
Under which painful memories, quietly flows!
A woman truly understands another,
She knows the sorrow of another's heart!

They console her, patting her gently
And promise her of her brother's coming.
Laughing like a brook, one moment,
Heavy and laden with sorrow's snow, next!

The downpour mingles with tears and flows
Sun and shadow's magic, touches, again her brow.
She is fire and ice! She is a candle's light!
She is life-giving warmth of a kitchen stove!

She is a warm heart, pulsating with love,
She gives a New life, blessed from above!
All this and still she is much more!

That makes the quilt of a woman's heart-

Ages have rolled and ages have gone,
Yet her "Mystery' upon this world, still holds!
Elusive she is, like the human emotions,
And all pervasive, as God's true blessings!

As the Nature's surety, she always stays,
Like the Earth itself, patient and fruitful!
The Monsoon winds are now here,
The seasons have finally changed,
The cycle of life so rhythmic rolls again

Regular in its cosmic dance!
The ritual of "Hanging the Swing"
On stout limbs of sturdy trees-
Where upon the beautiful Maidens swing
And sing the melodious songs of Hind—

They remember their loves and pains,

How with their 'beloved', they had lain—
The fulfillment of their very lives,
As daughters silently, turned to wives!

Says one now to another, "Listen,
O my childhood's sweet friend!
Every year I will come over here,
To sing and swing with you in rain!"

"How wonderful it is to come back
To our restful, childhood homes!
Here, there are no worries for me,
And there are no boring chores!"

"I have come, visiting my mother!
She now takes care of my child!
While I swing on this Monsoon Swing
Sing and chat and laugh awhile!"

"My father seems older now to me,

For it's my brother who tills our soil—
O how my father, dots on my son,
Staying here, I know, he will get spoilt!"
"My brother's wife is so gracious to me,
She never allows me to cook—
She dishes out hot meals for me,
Every day, tirelessly, it helps me heal!"

The innocent gossip goes on under the shade,
Of who got wed and who was left behind—
Who ran away with whom, what a shame!
Surely this world is coming to its end!

Soon the Monsoon clouds will roll on,
Emptying all that they hold in store
Within their dark bosom, they hold so much,
Emptied, they will thunder and rant no more—

One says reminiscing to the other,
"Listen friend! It was the last monsoon,

I had been wed, the year before

And my husband would hold me so close!"

He wouldn't allow me to come back here,

To my father's home, he wouldn't let me come!

Our love was young and flame aglow,

O how many thunders, we both endured!"

I remember the night sky

Dark and forbidding and starless,

As it thundered and boomed above,

And lightening streaked across the sky!

I shivered and trembled, he held,

Me, in his arms, all night, as we lay,

He stroked my head and kissed my brow,

Wrapped me in his wonderful love, so slow"—

As she remembered her lover,

She blushed and hid her face,

Into her soft palms and then prayed,

"O mighty Winds! Take my breath to him!"

The other girls laughed at her tale,
"Come, come, you love-sick child-
Soon you'll be united with your mate"

Said one, who was on in years!

She spoke from past experience-
As she also had felt all that some time,
The young love and its fulfillment,
Loving another soul, at heart's content!

"Girls! Now we had enough of play!
Come, let us go yonder and pray!
Let us ask God, of good things,
Love, life and upon children, Blessings!"

Thus, ordered the eldest one of all
Swiftly they all obliged and rolled.
The Swings were abandoned, all at once!
The awakened flowers lay trodden in dust!

The girls left quickly, as they had come
The silent bough and empty swings just stared!

A swing still swayed, lamely in breeze,
The scene suddenly turned still life in freeze.
Now silence ruled on the 'Golden Bough',
The swings stood hanging, empty in a row!
The monsoon clouds then roared so low!

Lighting just then ran across dark skies,
The Old Banyan tree, lay now deserted
It had seen many a 'season's play!'
The 'shepherd boy' went on his way

Now the girls had quit their 'play'
The clouds burst open into the rain!

The whole world lay drenched in pain!
Now the monsoon season had begun,
Like the song from a maiden's lip, in fun!

Monsoon Swing

"The monsoon swings and the flowered bough,

The fragrant air and the sensuous play now,

The maidens so lovely, so tender and rare,

Pray to you, come back next year and play!"

~~~~~~~~~~~~~~~~~~~~~~~

Love Travels

When my eyes turn to birds,
And fly across the seas
And come to you my beloved,
To sit on your Mango tree!
I sit there my love and
Clean my feathers green,
The water beads drop down,
Unto the dust below!
I open my red beak and sing
And shout aloud your name,
You look at me and smile,
That springy look on your face
And yawn and spread
Your wide arms, above your head!
That sight of yours, like
A stretching panther, in glee,
I will remember, always!

~~~~~~~~*^*~~~~~~~~~

Eulogy

Ah! You are so far away,

It almost feels unreal,

That I can love you so,

But you are nowhere near!

Yet, in my memories,

You'll always be mine ---

When I remember our love,

Only tenderness will shine!

With my slowly growing self

I still hide a light inside ---

That burns inside in me

And doesn't know no freight!

Go away my beloved,

Forever denied to me

But make a happy life,

For all the world to see!

This is my last farewell

In my silent thoughts,

A bow to our memories

A veil on our love!

****

Your Name

Every now and then

I pick up pieces that,

I had left all around me

And, wait---

Putting something off

In a far corner of mind,

Till once again, they

Rush on from behind!

Needless to say,

How much pain they bring,

When I put all pieces in one,

And still, a corner is missing!

Ah! That last corner,

Where you put your name!

~~~~~~~~*^*~~~~~~~~~

I Will Return (JE REVINS)

And when the tear, silently creeps away,

Wrenched out of the heart, it slips away,

A river running out of my memories it is,

At those times, I feel, I love you still!

My lonely love come back to me!

Come to me, the same way again ------

One by one, so unexpectedly to roll

On my warm cheek, down the slope to fall

Then on the bosom, it silently falls!

How is it that these innocent tears of an hour

Bring so much peace to my heart today?

~~~~~~~~~~~^*^~~~~~~~~~~~~~~~~~~

Night Traveler

Who walks the empty night?

As alone as I?

Whose footsteps clatter by?

Restless same as mine?

O my silent friend,

You too cannot sleep?

I know what the agony is

Of your tired mind-----

This silent you break,

Measuring with your walk,

But tread softly my friend,

For rest of the world still sleeps!

This loneliness and memories

Are all that we have?

This long night and darkness,

Are only ours to share!

~~~~~~~~^*^~~~~~~~~~~~~~

Rose Bush

Oh! For my belated marriage,

How many blooms I give!

Each day with a fresh rose on bush,

Of my emotions, I smile!

Then the Rose, withers away—

In the hands of merciless Time!

The sweet smell of a rose

As poignant as a longing

Trails behind, filling the bough

And the garden around!

Like a solitary figure on rocks,

Clad in phantom memories,

Besides a vast breaking sea!

~~~~~~~~~~^~~~~~~~~~~~

Rain

Again, it will come, the season
That drizzling world of downpour,
But we won't be together anymore!
And then again will come rains!
The same desperate drops, on sand,
The same earthy smell shall rise,
And the thick curtain of rain
Will tremble lift and fall with a sigh!
Unbroken chain of droplets
Spread like the mysterious night,
Far away, a tiny flicker,
Lost in the water's howling crest!
How can it fight the ferocity?
Impounding fury, so bare, so raw?
My heart pounds with a boom
Thunder then echo's my song!
Lightening then streaks, across the sky
Wet is the world and wet am I!

Memories My Love

When I write poems for you,

I see, only black and white

I put my hands over it

And see that lonely smile---

Somehow, they seem like a caress!

As though with the breezes,

From some sandy shores,

Some sea salt and some air,

Had slipped along your hair—

As the waves ruffle the ocean

My hands caress your hair

So much and harmony

They gave us then to share!

~~~~~~~~^*^~~~~~~~~~~~

Seasons

The snow promises

The coming of spring

The spring that of summer!

Summer's heat beckons autumn

And autumn turns to winter!

The ever-changing cycle

We face with such surety!

As days turn to nights,

And darkness turns to dawn!

Nothing remains the same, forever,

Yet everything looks the same!

A child grows everyday

And a youth becomes a man!

A man will surely age then,

And an old man will surely die!

Who has set all these patterns?

Who controls ebb and tides?

Who paints the sky above?

And who lends the colors below?

Who fashions each blade and dale?

Who paints the merry flowers?

Who fashioned this world around us?

Who silently smiles and hides?

Who gave me eyes to see all this?

And ears to hear sweet melodies?

Who gave me love and life?

Who gave laughter and smiles?

Why tears flow from memories,

Why pain brings forth new pain?

What then men strive to gain?

In the whirling, churning flow

I try to grasp some straws!

These are my understandings—

For the riddles of life's flows.

~~~~~~~~~ *~~~~~~~~~~~~~~~~~~~~~~~

Memories

The eyes heavy with memories
With silver spools spilling by
The eyes my love, just wants to see
You, my love and cry!
It is easy to say that
'Parting is such a sweet sorrow'
But the love I found with you says,
'You and me, beneath the bough
And wilderness is paradise now!'
My memories are made of them
And that last time you looked at me,
Your locked gaze, moved away from me
And there, so helpless I stood!
Will I ever forget all this?
For in every face, that is,
Fraught with pain, I see you,
The way I saw you last-
You fuse with every pain in me—

And stay, forever, within my heart!

For I know that this happened

Again, and again in my life.

Experiences and love and pain

And my love and yours are still alive!

When did you stop, or I could stop?

For what had you, or I done

That was even a little wrong?

So we never blamed one another, nor

Stopped loving one another.

Memories, my love, burns inside me still

And gives me new insight!

~~~~~~~~~~~~~~~~~~~~~~~~~~~~~~~`

Always

Is it a sin to say that I love you?

In the hoard of merriment in life

Of mine and others,

The sudden pain of partition, of death,

I ask you about yourself, of myself

I tell you --- always!

What remains in mind, is a frosty night,

A silent night in forest of white,

Only, white!

There you move for me,

Outside the window, a shadowy figure,

Can't see you, but try, indeed I do!

What do I try to hold?

In my grasp that slips,

Like the sands of time

Running out fast from life!

I count your breath

And my cold one too –

Oh! To mingle together,

Until end to last!

'Be secure and warm –

Have life and norm –

Yet do whatever that,

Pleases you always!'

Always! always – yes,

There is going to be

An always - - even after,

Yes – there will be always!

~~~~~~~~~~~~~~~~~~~~~~~~~`

Spirit

For my pride, for myself

For simply being alive

To know the joy of life

To experience love and pain,

What? Oh, What I won't give?

Everything that belong to me

All my years and time

Filled with dread and grief

And tired body and mind –

All these, yes, I can bear

But O my heart, you stay free!

Free as a bird, up in the sky,

Soaring upward, bring cold from there!

I shall cherish all these

And save them in my memories

For all the coming grey times

And for shadows that grow long

When the end of life comes

Then, I'll be just that,

So barely alive, so withered will be I!

But yes, my spirit and heart

Shall have learnt some more

Keeping company with me

With my tired and old self – Oh!

Yes! It'll surely be there!

~~~~~~~~~~~~~~~~~~~~~~~~~~~`

All Alone Without You

At the eve of my utmost triumph
You are not with me my love!
When I bask in the thunder
Of the deafening applause, you aren't here!
I look at all the upturned faces,
Look at happy smiles, running out to me,
Yet I see, only emptiness inside!
My search for you has not yet begun
Yet you have gone far away –
How I could I last, without you?
I am standing alone, by myself, my love!
Will you come to me again, my man?
Or do I have to be forever, lonely?

~~~~~~~~~~~~~~~~~~~~~~~~~~~~

Diwali

(November 13, 1975)

Today how I feel?

In a new land with new people?

Life remains the same, but

Living it is somehow different!

In all corners of this world

There is separate Universe

For all people concerned!

The festival of Lights, comes hither,

Shining softly, it advances ahead,

Filling the night with an amber glow!

Bright like my eyes,

Filled with expectancy and joy!

Come, come my Beloved,

For all this spread is for you!

All the lights are for you

All the joys are for you!

My life and my love are for you!

Me, and my Fisher Woman!

Today, I hear voices, rising from closed doors,

As if the waves on a sleeping sea,

Have sprung unto life!

Today again my lamp of pleasure lights,

The night is passing by,

In its softly burning light!

The muffled song of life, as dim as the lamp,

Which hangs up on the mast?

Fighting the grim darkness!

My boat rocks, goes ahead and stops,

The sea slaps it, to and fro,

Awakening and putting it to sleep!

There is one light with me, brightness in life,

Fixed forever, like the North Star,

Like my tested faith in God!

I am a sailor, standing, watching the sea,

My lamp and the sleeping, companion of mine!

Hush! Don't awake her, she sleeps –

Lost in the dark night, exhausted,

She lies like dead, in the journey of night!

We, with our childish innocence,

And no desire, to find a neither shore nor destiny!

Nay – we don't want them ---

We two are wanderers wild!

I have come to find fairway,

A land that is Heaven,

On the other side of the seas!

Beyond horizon – a small corner –

One corner, where we will live,

Two souls, all alone, wrapped in love,

Me and my Fisherwoman!

We would live like the exiled King and Queen,

In a lush green cottage, besides the sea,

A bed, fish and my boat within,

Vicinity and in front, the sea!

In all its glory, fuming so blue!

Then sand will come running from all sides,

To capture the dancing sea in its arms!

At night fall, me and my friend the woman

Would watch the lamp on the mast,

The sea from the shore, we would see,

And we would sit, side by side there,

Me, and my Fisher woman!

Me, and my Fisher Woman!

Sword

Tense as the edge of a steel blade
Or like a sharp sword, hanging above,
Overhead, from there, and I cannot move!
I stand there, mute, devoid of senses
With the deepest influences and
Impressions, creeping all over me –
Me, the receiver is full to the brim
Hung on a thin thread, on edge,
I stand under a ready Sword!
Now it'll strike and now it'll fall
It'll kill me, oh, here I go!
It'll crash the world around me!
I'm doomed! Am ready to scream
My eyes are fixed with a mad gleam,
Fascinated, transfixed, I still stand,
This devotion only death commands!
Don't think these are songs of sorrow,
Or despair or melancholy or lost love –

I'm optimistic and gay, as can be, but,

The question remains still unanswered –

The killer out too long, loose to kill!

Strike! Strike! It will strike! It surely will!

~~~```````````````~~~~

Conversation

(Christmas, Dec 25, 1974)

Yes, I have also loved brother,

Yes, I have also loved!

I have known the warm bed,

The deep sighs of contentment,

Of the pain pulling at heart,

When the shadow parts –

Then only a memory remains!

I have longed for warmth,

Longed for strong arms holding me tight,

Of deep sighs and feelings pure

Of never letting out of sight!

Yes, the pain comes with partition

The world has to move ahead

There is bliss and there is grief

Until blood race and heart prevail!

I have known the moment

When mouths were shut and eyes spoke,

And fingers touched and locked in a grip
And the soft pressure would then say
'I love you still' that lips needn't say!
Ah! How the shadows brushed,
And moved away then open smiles
Would touch the lips and say,
'I love you still' that lit up the face!
Yes, I have also loved brother,
Yes, I have also loved!
When hearts talk in a language
Of universal peace and joy,
Deep satisfaction and contentment,
Of mighty joys and pains –
Yes! I have also loved brother,
Yes, I have also loved!
I remember the days and nights,
Those frosty nights and clear days
The nightingale and the sparrow's chirp
And howling winds on flowing scents!
They come to me, all of it

Riding high waves on surf
Gliding through snow, on sleighs,
And riding on the wings of birds!
The phantom of my memories,
Of loves and moments lost,
Of death and of pain in heart,
And of farewell of a friend!
Of solitude and silent unions,
Of love, of life and worship
And belonging for a lifetime!
Yes! I have also loved brother,
I have also loved!

--------------- * ---------------

Love is Immortal
(Jan 9, 1975)

If you were a king and I your slave,

Would you love me still?

Oh! If you were a king!

How easy for you to call me would be,

For I was meant to serve,

Will you buy my heart or

Will you buy my soul?

Oh! If you were a King and I your slave

Would you love me still?

The love would come

And slowly blossom

Like the shiny petals of a windswept rose

And I would tremble at your touch

Yet you would hold me still!

Oh! If you were a king and I your slave,

Would you love me still?

And Ah! For your kisses,

Pure as the breeze
I would open my arms,
And hold you within
Until we melt and kiss!
Oh! If you were a king and I your slave,
Would you love me still?
So full of love,
The sunshine would be,
Like your smiles, yes,
Smile, eternally at me!
Ah! If you were a king and I your slave,
Would you love me still?
If you were a king, I won't bow down,
To you, or to your laws,
Nor to your guards,
Who may hold me fast?
Nor to your overflowing kingdom –
Nor to your family
Nor kith nor kin
Friends or Foe-oh no!

Ah! If you were a king and I your slave,

Would you love me still?

I would stand erect

With my unkempt hair

Gaze steadily at you,

You, my monarch,

And forgive you, your sins!

What would be my death?

Just a slave's replacement!

Oh! If you were a king and I your slave,

Would you love me still?

I live for your love,

I pine for the same

I breathe your love,

And want your joy

A life, rich with love

With everlasting bliss

And pain so sharp

Which only would go

When we were no more!

Yet, we shall be gone

But our love will remain!

Oh! If you were a king and I your slave,

Will you love me still?

Only love will remain

A legend will grow

Is there death to souls?

If you were a king and I your slave,

Our poignant tale will remain

It'll be sung for centuries—

It'll be a legacy to the world,

For lovers like us,

For hopes in future

For hurdles and time

When two true hearts unite –

Their love will join in our song

Their voices shall regain,

Their youth, through what they sing

And in them we shall unite!

In heaven we shall hear,

These immortal songs and say,

Oh! If you were a king and I your slave,

Will you love me still?

Say, would you love me still?

~~~~~~~~~~~~~~

India

(January 26 1974)

I bring you the songs of joy,

From a land far off—India!

Where still the heart prevails,

Over technical skill and media!

Brown is the earth

Fruits and flowers fresh,

Orchids you will find here,

In this wild and untouched land!

It is a sleeping country still

Where people take their time,

In moving about and even,

Saying to you 'goodbye!'

Yes! They cling to you with love,

With feelings of gratitude and care,

And doesn't humanity want only this,

Whatever bold and uncaring it may say?

The innocent people live their lives,

In simple tricks and harmony
And are happy with their simple lives!
You may call them high-handedly
'Yes, ignorance is bliss!'

And was not man, so happy then,
When Adam had his Eve?
No big crusades they want –
No huge achievements in life
Nor great luxuries nor
Rapid advancements and
All that which strip his humanity!
Yes – that will be an Indian!
A man from an ancient land
The sages leave behind the world
To seek permanent bliss
The higher values and deeper meanings
The mastery of Yoga they seek.
On reaching the pinnacle
Of his manhood and energy

They find the total bliss!

NIRVANA! For an Indian is

His life's eternal quest!

Yes! This is the true India

The old forgotten land!

Ah Hope!

When shall they meet?

Ah Hope! Who have parted today, when shall they meet?

From today, the Lovebirds, shall be called the seers of love,

Ah! Hope, who have parted today, when shall they meet?

If a fraction of a second, could be mine, in my dreams,

With you and if only it were true,

But alas! For this hopeless penance!

Ah! Hope! Who have parted today, when shall they meet?

For I know that, we will never meet,

But spring will roll on and Monsoon occur,

Look at me at your hearts content,

For I shall never return –

Ah Hope! Who have parted today, when shall they meet?

Cry no more, your tears are futile

Teach your heart to be able to laugh

But to laugh together, we won't meet!

Ah Hope! Who have parted today, when shall they meet?

From today, shall we see, same stars in the sky?

But apart, forever, like two riverbanks,

Which do not meet, even at the sea!

Ah Hope! Who have parted today, when shall they meet?

Like the broken halves of a heart,

Lay, the two river sides, prostrate, helpless,

Dividing them, flows the River of Time –

On this path of beginning and End!

They won't ever meet –

Ah Hope! Who have parted today, when shall they meet?

If only I were sure, that I could

Meet you, Beloved, in Heaven,

I wouldn't be so helpless

But will we meet, even in dreams?

Ah Hope! Who have parted today, when shall they meet?

There was no dreamer, whose dreams came true,

The hazy hands of dreams never,

Wipe out the hands of Destiny!

Now I know, it is impossible to meet!

Ah Hope! Who have parted, when shall they meet?

Ah! That last night of our union,

You sat close to me, your head

Was on my shoulder, your hair, wild,

And asked in a thin voice of me,

"When shall we meet?"

When I, soaked in sorrow, ask,

The world around, "When shall I meet?"

"When shall I meet?" echoes,

The space and the sea in a scream!

The answer to the question, the same!

Ah Hope! Who have parted today, when shall they meet?

...

Don't blunt the fine edge of the sword of my life,

Don't fill the cup to the brim, for it'll fall!

Luxuries of life, of senses,

What shall I do with you?

...

Every age of Prophet

Passes away from us,

Only their memories

Lingers then for us!

O! My kind Fathers,

Do forgive us, our sins!

America (A Prayer)

Give me the quiet strength of your soil,

Give me the will to reach for the moon!

Give me the toil of desperate limbs,

Give me the shocks and horrors of sins!

Give me the bravery of your braves –

Give me the affection, for motherland!

Give me your love, your benevolence --

Give me your true and noble spirit!

America! The most wonders land!

A free nation! Undivided! And one!

From Alaska to Hawaii ---

From New York to Los-Angeles,

From Mexico to Canada, you lie,

From Sea to shining Sea!

Old Glory flutters high up in the sky

Multitudes of masses go rushing by –

May God keep you, safe and sound!

No adversaries, nor enemies, come around!

Your wondrous bounty, may know no bounds!

Amen!

Love

I met you, at that perfect time of life,

Just as a season, passing on from cold,

Thaws and blossoms forth into a spring!

As crossroads and currents collide

On a muddy path or on an ocean's bosom,

"You" met me, at those, cross- currents of life!

Just as a youth, enters his adulthood,

Tiptoeing comes promises of a new life,

"You" came! As the night recedes,

And a new dawn emerges, breaking into a day

and when the evening shadows linger

On the painted horizon, for just a little while!

As the Jasmine bud opens with longing

And the silent night, watches it in awe,

As the cool breeze of the night awaits.

The first fragrance mingles into the night!

A bud becomes a flower and life unfolds.

Who sings a song of joy on that bough above!

"You" and all the things, that surrounds me,

Nature and God, in His splendor

All are enmeshed into a web of gossamer,

An interlinking design, woven in soft silk!

That invisible link, linking us all alike,

Is – and always will be, LOVE, that unites!

~~~~~~~~~~~~~~~~~

Aah! the gypsy sings

Aah! the gypsy sings ...
When the gypsy sings from my soul,
My lips sweetly call out your name!
The long-hidden magic unwinds
On scented night breeze,
Aah! the gypsy sings....

The sounds go back centuries,
but rise from hidden depths of me
My soul yearns, those passionate nights,
when we met, beneath Flame tree.
... Aah! the gypsy sings ...

Our eyes met, hands locked,
then embrace, you held me tight
till my breath was lost
your trembling lips upon my brow
and held me so, to crush my soul

Aah! the gypsy sings ...

These songs that have been sung by me,
have been sung, again and again, by many
past is present and present is past
future will come on a broad impasse
Aah! the gypsy sings ...

The songs that break the silence
surely come from some unseen
the caravan of life flickers and moves,
under magic lanterns burning bright!
Aah! the gypsy sings ...

Tonight, as I sing so you too will,
and countless others over distant seas,
over hills and dales their echoes rise,
filling the night with stars that shine
Aah! the gypsy sings ...
The gypsy sings... The gypsy sings

About Long Poem

Q: what is a Long Poem?

A: some interesting facts related to long poem are given below. The long poem is a literary genre including all poetry of considerable length.

Though the definition of a long poem is vague and broad, the genre includes some of the most important poetry ever written.

The long poem has evolved into an umbrella term, encompassing many sub genres, including epic, verse novel, verse narrative, lyric sequence, lyric series, and collage/montage.

Q: Which is the longest poem of world?

A: With more than 220000 (100000 shloka or couplets) verses and about 1.8 million words in total, the Mahābhārata is the longest epic poem in the world.

It is roughly ten times the size of the Iliad and Odyssey which was written by Homer in ancient Greek literature combined. Epic poem Mahabharat is five times longer than Dante's Divine Comedy which is a long Italian narrative poem by Dante Alighieri, and four times the size of the Indian epic Ramayana and Ferdowsi's Shahnameh.

In English, Beowulf and Chaucer's Troilus and Criseyde are among the first important long poems. The long poem thrived and gained new vitality in the hands of experimental Modernists in the early 1900s and has continued to evolve through the 21st century.

A long poem often functions to tell a "tale of the tribe", or a story that encompasses a whole culture's values and history.

Ezra Pound coined the phrase, " tale of the tribe" referring to his own long poem The Cantos. Walt Whitman tried to achieve this idea of characterizing the American identity in Song of Myself. Elizabeth Barrett Browning was one of the first female authors to attempt an epic poem. In her article "Written in blood: the art of mothering epic in the poetry of Elizabeth Barrett Browning", Olivia Gatti Taylor explores Browning's attempt to write an authentically feminine epic poem titled Aurora Leigh.

Romantic long poem:
The critic Lilach Lachman describes the Romantic long poem as one that, "questioned the coherence of the conventional epic's plot. Also, its logic of time and space, and its laws of interconnecting the narrative through action."

Examples of the Romantic long poem is Keats' long poem Hyperion: A Fragment (1820), William Wordsworth's Recluse (Including the Prelude (1850), and The Excursion), and Percy Bysshe Shelley's Prometheus Unbound. In India a yogi & a poet Aurobindo wrote Sri Savitri a long poem in 1951.

The best-known Bengali long poem is JAKHAM (The Wound) written by Malay Roy Choudhury of India during the famous Hungryalist movement in 1960s.

The long poem's length and scope can contain concerns of a magnitude that a shorter poem cannot address. The poet may see himself or herself as the "bearer of the light", to use Langston Hughes' term, who leads the journey through a culture's story, or as the one who makes known the light already within the tribe.

The poet may also serve as a poet-prophet with special insight for their own tribe.

- Lavanya Deepak Shah

Cover Artist

Susheela Narendra Sharma

The artwork on cover page of *Monsoon Swing and Other Poems* is from a painting titled 'Abhisarika' by poetess Lavanya Shah's mother **Mrs. Susheela Narendra Sharma**. She was a student of fine arts at Haldenkar Institute in Mumbai, India.

This method of watercolor painting is called 'wash method'.

In this painting of a female holding a tree limb as she holds a water pot - the portion of lower garment of saree of the female depicted as the subject has the original art paper which has been left untouched while rest of the painting is saturated with watercolor paints painstakingly, again and again then washed with a sponge, and re-painted with water colors on the original art paper. Thus, achieving the soft patina of colors which retains its beauty on the finished artwork painting.

Author's Biodata

Lavanya Deepak Shah

Daughter of a renowned thinker, poet, lyricist, and freedom fighter Pt. Narendra Sharma, Lavanya Shah is a well-known Hindi poet. She was born in Mumbai, India. She lives in the USA since 1989.

Lavanya Shah has written four books in Hindi which include a novel, a collection of poems, a collection of short stories and poetic interpretation of Sunder-Kaand from Ramcharit Manas of Saint Tulasidas.

'Songs from Monsoon Swings and Other Poems' is her first book in English language.

Songs from a Monsoon Swing and Other Poems

www.ingramcontent.com/pod-product-compliance
Lightning Source LLC
Chambersburg PA
CBHW070627050426
42450CB00011B/3134